CPSIA information can be obtained
at www.ICGtesting.com
Printed in the USA
BVHW060741171222
654411BV00019B/1055

آفَت کی ضِیافَت

یاور ماجد

AAFAT KI ZIYAAFAT

Yawar Maajed

Shh..... Secret Surpise in the QR Code below

TITLE:	Aafat Ki Ziyaafat
AUTHOR:	Yawar Maajed
ILLUSTRATIONS:	Franco Farias (MrKatMan)
PUBLISHED BY:	GhazalSara.Org
PUBLISHED:	December 2022
ISBN:	978-1-957756-10-3
CONTACT:	ghazalsara.org@outlook.com
EDITION:	Standard Color Paperback Edition

Available in color paperback and premium color hardcover gift edition in the entire world.

Look for eBook too on Apple Books, Google Playbooks or any other eBook store. On Apple Books, it contains music too.

Printed and bound in the U.S.A.

بَڑی آفَت کی مَیں نے کی ضِیافَت

baRi aafat ki maiN ne ki ziyafat

ذَرا سا گَرْم تھوڑا کوسا کوسا
دِیا کھانے کو کھوسہ کو سَموسہ

zara sa garm thoRa kosa kosa
diya khane ko khosa ko samosa

نَہ دانتوں پَر کِیا اُس نے بھَروسا

na dantoN par kiya us ne bharosa

سَموسَہ اُس نے جا کانوں میں ٹھونسَا

samosa us ne ja kanoN meiN Thonsa

سَموسے کو کِیا یُوں اُس نے غارَت

بَڑی آفَت کی مَیں نے کی ضِیافَت

samose ko kiya yuN us ne GHaarat
baRi aafat ki maiN ne ki ziyafat

لَگایا گھَر میں مَیں نے خُوب میلہ

lagaya ghar meiN maiN ne KHoob mela

چَڑھایا پہلے اِک ٹھیلے پہ لیلا

chaRhaya pehle ik Thele pe lela

پھِر اُس کو نِیم کے نِیچے دَھکیلا

phir us ko neem ke neeche dhakela

اور اُس کے منْہ میں اِک ڈالا کریلا

aur us ke munh meiN ik Daala karela

نہ لی اُس سے کوئی مَیں نے اِجازَت

بَڑی آفَت کی مَیں نے کی ضِیافَت

na li us se koyi maiN ne ijazat
baRi aafat ki maiN ne ki ziyafat

مَلی چِہرے پہ جا دَجّال کے دال

mali chehre pe ja dajjaal ke daal

تو اُس کے مُنہ سے بہنے لَگ پَڑی رال

to us ke munh se behne lag paRi raal

نِکل آیا مَگر پھِر دال سے بال

nikal aaya magar phir daal se baal

اُتاری خُوب اُس نے بال کی کھال

utaari KHoob us ne baal ki khaal

دِکھائی اِس طَرَح مَیں نے شُجاعَت

بَڑی آفَت کی مَیں نے کی ضِیافَت

dikhayi is tarha maiN ne shuja'at
baRi aafat ki maiN ne ki ziyafat

کُتَرتا تھا کھَڑا جو لان میں نان

kutarta tha khaRa jo lawn meiN naan

جو گانے کو ہُوا جاتا تھا ہَلکان

jo gaane ko hua jaata tha halkaan

دِیا گُونگے سے اُس مہْمان کو پان

diya guNge se us mehman ko paan

کُترنے وہ لگا خود اپنے ہی کان

کُترنے میں تھی اُس کے اِک نَزَاکت

kutarne vo laga KHud apne hi kaan
kutarne meiN thi us ke ik nazakat

بَڑی آفَت کی مَیں نے کی ضِیافَت

baRi aafat ki maiN ne ki ziyafat

عَجَب گَڑ بَڑ ہے ہَڑ ہَڑ کا مُرَبّہ

ajab gaR baR hai haR haR ka murabba

مُرَبّے کا جو کھولا مَیں نے ڈَّبہ

murabbe ka jo khola maine Dabba

لَگا کپڑوں پہ میرے ایک دَھبّہ

laga kapRoN pe mere ek dhabba

تو میرے پِیچھے دَوڑے میرے ابّا

to mere peeche dauRe mere abba

سَمَجھ لو آ گئی میری بھی شامَت

بَڑی آفَت کی مَیں نے کی ضِیافَت

samjh lo aa gayi meri bhi shaamat
baRi aafat ki maiN ne ki ziyafat

دی اِک گھوڑی نِگوڑی کو پَکوڑی

di ik ghoRi nigoRi ko pakoRi

پَکوڑی اُس نے دانتوں سے بھَنبھوڑی

pakoRi us ne daantoN se bhaNbhoRi

مَگر مِرچیں لَگیں جَب اُس کو تھوڑی

magar mircheiN lageeN jab us ko thoRi

تو گھوڑی سَر پہ پاؤں رَکھ کے دوڑی

to ghoRi sar pe paaoN rakh ke dauRi

ضِیافَت گھوڑی نے کر ڈالی غارَت
بَڑی آفَت کی مَیں نے کی ضِیافَت

ziyafat ghoRi ne kar Daali GHaarat
baRi aafat ki maiN ne ki ziyafat

جو مَکڑی مَیں نے اَپنے سَر سے پَکڑی

jo makRi maiN ne apne sar se pakRi

اُسے نہْلایا اور پہنائی پَگڑی

use nehlaya aur pehnayi pagRi

کِھلائی اُس کو پِھر تَگڑی سی ککڑی

khilayi us ko phir tagRi si kakRi

تو مَکڑی نے وہ ککڑی مُجھ سے جَکڑی

to makRi ne vo kakRi mujh se jakRi

تھی مَکڑی کے جَکڑنے میں نَفاسَت

بَڑی آفَت کی مَیں نے کی ضِیافَت

thi makRi ke jakaRne meiN nafaasat

baRi aafat ki maiN ne ki ziyafat

نَظَر آیا جو بھَینگا ایک جھِینگا

nazar aaya jo bhaiNga ek jheeNga

دِکھایا مَیں نے اُس جھِینگے کو ٹھِینگا

dikhaya maiN ne us jheeNge ko TheeNga

وہ پہلے تو زَمیں پَر تھوڑا رِینگا

vo pehle to zameeN par thoRa reeNga

مَگر کرنے لَگا پِھر مُجھ سے دھِینگا

magar karne laga phir mujh se dheeNga

دِکھائی دھِینگے میں مَیں نے مَہارَت

بَڑی آفَت کی مَیں نے کی ضِیافَت

dikhayi dheeNge meiN maiN ne mahaarat
baRi aafat ki maiN ne ki ziyafat

کِھلائے خالُو کو آلُو وِنڈالُو

khilaaye KHaalu ko aalu vinDalu

تو آ دھَمکا وَہاں کالُو سا بھالُو

تھا جِس کا نام بھُونچالُو گَچالُو

to aa dhamka vahaN kaalu sa bhaalu
tha jis ka naam bhooNchalu kachalu

چَبائے بھَالُو نے تالُو سے آلُو

chabaaye bhaalu ne taalu se aalu

غَٹا غَٹ پی گیا پھِر ڈھیر شَربَت

GHaTa GHaT pee gaya phir dher sharbat

بَڑی آفَت کی مَیں نے کی ضِیافَت

baRi aafat ki maiN ne ki ziyafat

مَچھَندَر نام کا تھا ایک بَندَر

machhandar naam ka tha ek bandar

بُلائے بِن جو آیا گھَر کے آندَر

bulaaye bin jo aaya ghar ke andar

اُٹھا مارا اُسے ایسے چِقَندَر

uTha maara use aise chiqandar

کہ بَندَر بَن گَیا جھَٹ سے قَلَندَر

ke bandar ban gaya jhaT se qalandar

مَچھَندَر کی ذَرا دیکھو سِیاسَت

بَڑی آفَت کی مَیں نے کی ضِیافَت

machhandar ki zara dekho siyasat
baRi aafat ki maiN ne ki ziyafat

وہ اِک سُنڈی جو تھی بالکُل ہی ٹِنڈی

vo ik sunDi jo thi bilkul hi TinDi

لَگائی سَر پہ اُس ٹِنڈی کے بھِنڈی

lagaayi sar pe us TinDi ke bhinDi

پکوڑے سَر پہ تھوڑے سے نِچوڑے

pakoRe sar pe thoRe se nichoRe

اُگا کر کھیت اُس کے سَر پہ چھوڑے

uga ker khet us ke sar pe chhoRe

وہ بھاگی کرنے بھِنڈی کی تِجارَت

بَڑی آفَت کی مَیں نے کی ضِیافَت

vo bhaagi karne bhinDi ki tijaarat
baRi aafat ki maiN ne ki ziyafat

ذَرا سی جاگی تھوڑی سوئی سوئی

zara si jaagi thoRi soyi soyi

عَفِیفَہ آئی اور آتے ہی روئی

afeefa aayi aur aate hi royi

نہیں تھے دانت اُس کے مُنہ میں کوئی

naheeN the daaNt us ke munh meiN koyi

تو مَیں نے لَسّی ڈوئی سے بِلوئی

to maiN ne lassi Doyi se biloyi

عَفِیفہ نے کی لَسّی پر قَناعَت

afeefa ne ki lassi par qana'at

بَڑی آفَت کی مَیں نے کی ضِیافَت

baRi aafat ki maiN ne ki ziyafat

گھُسائے ناک میں پنسِل کا رَبَّڑ

چَلا آیا وَہاں اِک شیر بَبَّڑ

ghusaaye naak meiN pencil ka rabbaR
chala aaya vahaN ik sher babbaR

لَگایا اُس کو مَیں نے ایک جھانپَڑ

lagaaya us ko maiN ne ek jhaaNpaR

گھُسایا مُنہ میں اُس کے ڈیڑھ پاپَڑ

ghusaaya munh meiN us ke deRh paapaR

ہوئی پھِر خُوب بَبَّرْ کی حَجامَت

huyi phir KHoob babbR ki hajaamat

بَڑی آفَت کی مَیں نے کی ضِیافَت

baRi aafat ki maiN ne ki ziyafat

سَبھی بولے تِری آیسی کی تَیسی

sabhi bole teri aisi ki taisi

مَگر میری رَہی، جَیسی تھی وَیسی

magar meri rahi jaisi thi vaisi

نہ پُوچھو کیا مَچَا ڈالی قَیامَت

na poochho kya macha Daali qayamt

بَڑی آفَت کی مَیں نے کی ضِیافَت

baRi aafat ki maiN ne ki ziyafat

ziyaafat Dictionary

#	Term	Definition
1.	**AAFAT**	hell of a
2.	**ZIYAAFAT**	feast/party
3.	**AAFAT KI ZIYAFAT**	hell of a feast/party
4.	**KOSA**	warm
5.	**BHAROSA**	trust
6.	**GHAARAT**	ruined
7.	**LELA**	lamb
8.	**DAJJAAL**	anti-christ, enemy of God
9.	**RAAL**	drooling
10.	**SHUJA'AT**	bravery
11.	**HALKAAN**	excited
12.	**NAZAKAT**	delicacy
13.	**MURABBA**	pickle
14.	**BHANBHORI**	mauled
15.	**GHAARAT**	ruined
16.	**PAGRI**	turban
17.	**KAKRI**	melon/cucumber
18.	**NAFAASAT**	purity, refinement
19.	**JHEENGA**	shrimp
20.	**THEENGA**	thumb
21.	**DHEENGA**	wrestling
22.	**MAHAARAT**	expertise
23.	**KHAALU**	Uncle, mother's brother in law
24.	**TAALU**	palette of mouth
25.	**CHIQANDAR**	beet root
26.	**QALANDAR**	mystic
27.	**SUNDI**	caterpillar
28.	**TIJAARAT**	trade
29.	**QANA'AT**	contentment, satisfied

All children books are available in Urdu, Hindi and Roman scripts, in premium color hard cover and standard color paperback.

1.	aafat ki ziyafat	Watch Puplu arrange a hell of a party and have fun with all unintended guests
2.	dhagRak chup chup (Upcoming)	Puplu is too sick to go to school, or is he?
3.	Puplu mera naam (Upcoming)	Puplu is innocent, but always getting accused of mischief by everyone.
4.	dekhe ga ek zamana (Upcoming)	Puplu is out for doing the impossible
5.	paagal lafz huye (Upcoming)	Puplu chewed his tongue and now his words have gone loco.

Dr. Seuss Translations (Upcoming)

6.	sitara payT sancheele	"The Sneeches"
7.	Loru Laala ji	"The Lorax"
8.	KHaraatu kahani	"Dr. Seuss Sleepbook"
9.	janam din mubaarak	"Happy Birthday To You"
10.	bat bhatangaR road per kya kya hua	"And to Think That I Saw It on Mulberry Street"

Adult Poetry

11.	aaNkh bhar aasmaan	A colleciton of Ghazals and Poems
12.	Kulliyat e Ghazal Mir Taqi Mir	This compilation comes with a unique twist.
13.	Kulliyat e Ghazal Mirza Ghalib	This compilation comes with a unique twist.

For Buying Options Visit
HTTPS://WWW.GHAZALSARA.ORG/BBY